# Egg Cookbook

## A Timeless Collection of Egg Recipes

By
BookSumo Press

Published by
http://www.booksumo.com

# LEGAL NOTES

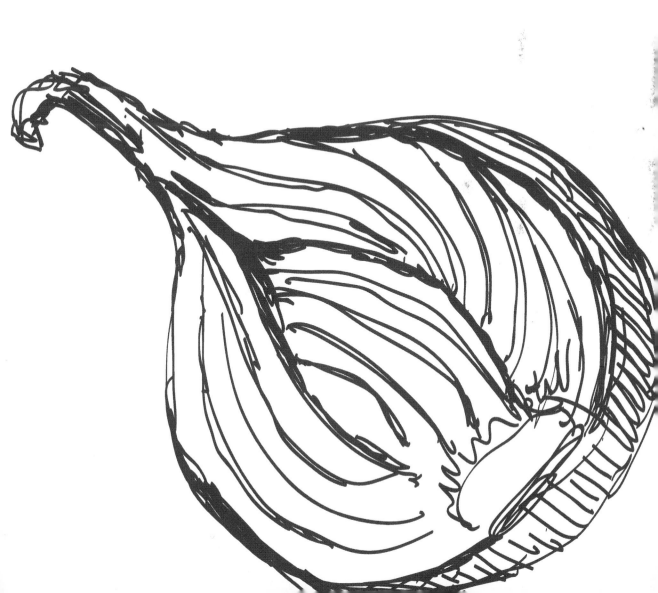

# Table of Contents

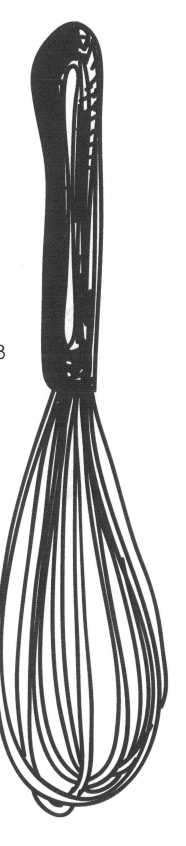

# *Parmesan* Zucchini Eggs

🥣 Prep Time: 10 mins
🕐 Total Time: 25 mins

Servings per Recipe: 4
| | |
|---|---|
| Calories | 147 kcal |
| Fat | 12.5 g |
| Carbohydrates | 1.6g |
| Protein | 7.6 g |
| Cholesterol | 188 mg |
| Sodium | 111 mg |

## Ingredients

4 eggs, lightly beaten
2 tbsps grated Parmesan cheese
2 tbsps olive oil
1 zucchini, sliced 1/8- to 1/4-inch thick

garlic powder, or to taste
salt and ground black pepper to taste

## Directions

1. Get a bowl, evenly mix: parmesan and whisked eggs.
2. Get a 2nd small bowl, combine in: pepper, garlic powder, and salt.
3. Fry your zucchini in olive oil for 8 mins. Pour in the seasonings from the 2nd bowl. Lower the heat and then pour in the first bowl.
4. Cook eggs for 4 mins. Turn off the heat and place a lid on the pan for 2 mins until the eggs are completely done

# EGGS
# in Bread

Prep Time: 10 mins
Total Time: 20 mins

Servings per Recipe: 1

| | |
|---|---|
| Calories | 189 kcal |
| Fat | 11.6 g |
| Carbohydrates | 13g |
| Protein | 8.3 g |
| Cholesterol | 201 mg |
| Sodium | 281 mg |

## Ingredients

1/2 tbsp butter
1 slice white bread
1 egg

## Directions

1. Coat your bread with butter on each of its sides. Then cut-out a circle in the middle of it.
2. Whisk your egg in a small bowl. Set it aside.
3. Get a skillet hot and for 1 min fry each side of the bread. Pour the egg into the hole and cook for 3 more mins.
4. Enjoy.

# A Quiche
# Of Mushrooms and Spinach

Prep Time: 15 mins
Total Time: 50 mins

| | |
|---|---|
| Servings per Recipe: 9 | |
| Calories | 325 kcal |
| Carbohydrates | 10.8 g |
| Cholesterol | 139 mg |
| Fat | 22.5 g |
| Protein | 20.9 g |
| Sodium | 806 mg |

## Ingredients

6 slices bacon
4 eggs, beaten
1 1/2 cups light cream
1/4 tsp ground nutmeg
1/2 tsp salt
1/2 tsp pepper
2 cups chopped fresh spinach

2 cups chopped fresh mushrooms
1/2 cup chopped onions
1 cup shredded Swiss cheese
1 cup shredded Cheddar cheese
1 (9 inch) deep dish pie crust

## Directions

1. Preheat your oven at 400 degrees F and put some oil over the quiche dish.
2. Cook bacon over medium heat until brown and then crumble it after draining.
3. Mix eggs, pepper, cream, salt, nutmeg, bacon, spinach, mushrooms, 3/4 cup Swiss cheese, 3/4 cup Cheddar cheese and onions in a bowl very thoroughly.
4. Pour this mixture over the pie crust and add some cheese.
5. Bake in the preheated oven for about 35 minutes or until the top of the quiche is golden brown in color.

# FRIED SAUSAGE
# and Eggs

Prep Time: 20 mins
Total Time: 30 mins

Servings per Recipe: 4

| | |
|---|---|
| Calories | 659 kcal |
| Fat | 53.9 g |
| Carbohydrates | 16.5g |
| Protein | 25.9 g |
| Cholesterol | 323 mg |
| Sodium | 1324 mg |

## Ingredients

1 lb beef sausage meat
2 tsps Worcestershire sauce
4 hard-cooked eggs, peeled
1 tbsp all-purpose flour
1/8 tsp salt

1/8 tsp ground black pepper
1 egg, whisked
2/3 cup dry bread crumbs
1 quart oil for deep frying

## Directions

1. Get a bowl, evenly mix: Worcestershire, pepper, sausage, salt and flour. Split the mix into four parts.
2. Wrap each of the four eggs with an equal part of sausage mix.
3. Get 2 bowls. Put whisked eggs into one bowl. Crumbled bread into another bowl. Coat each wrapped egg first with whisked eggs then dip into the bread.
4. Get some oil hot to 365 degrees in a large skillet, saucepan, or fryer and cook the eggs in the oil for 6 mins.

# *Tomato*
# Feta Eggs

Prep Time: 10 mins
Total Time: 15 mins

Servings per Recipe: 4

| | |
|---|---|
| Calories | 116 kcal |
| Fat | 8.9 g |
| Carbohydrates | 2g |
| Protein | 7.2 g |
| Cholesterol | 198 mg |
| Sodium | 435 mg |

## Ingredients

1 tbsp butter ~ 20 gm
1/4 cup chopped onion 60 ml
4 eggs, beaten
1/4 cup chopped tomatoes 60 ml

2 tbsps crumbled feta cheese ~ 40 gm
salt and pepper to taste

## Directions

1. Fry onions until see-through, in butter, in a frying pan. Then mix in your eggs. While the eggs are frying make sure to stir them so that they become scrambled.
2. Before the eggs are completely cooked add in your pepper and salt, then your feta, and finally your tomatoes.
3. Continue to let the eggs fry until the feta melts.

# EGGS
# from France

Prep Time: 10 mins
Total Time: 30 mins

Servings per Recipe: 8
| | |
|---|---|
| Calories | 336 kcal |
| Fat | 20.1 g |
| Carbohydrates | 25g |
| Protein | 13.2 g |
| Cholesterol | 252 mg |
| Sodium | 413 mg |

## Ingredients

1/2 cup butter
1/2 cup flour
salt and pepper to taste
1 quart milk
8 slices white bread, toasted

8 hard-cooked eggs
1 pinch paprika

## Directions

1. First get a saucepan hot before doing anything else.
2. Enter your butter into the saucepan and let it melt completely.
3. Then add in your flour, stir it a bit, and let it cook for 10 mins until it becomes lighter in colour.
4. Mix in your milk and wait until everything is lightly boiling, then set the heat to low.
5. Let it cook for 10 more mins.
6. Add in some pepper and salt.
7. Remove the yolks from each egg. Then you want to dice the egg whites and mix them into the simmering sauce.
8. Get a strainer and press the eggs through it. Put this in a bowl.
9. Put half a cup of simmering sauce on a piece of toasted bread and garnish the bread with the yolks and some paprika.
10. Enjoy.

# Romano
# and Pepperoni Eggs

Prep Time: 10 mins
Total Time: 20 mins

Servings per Recipe: 2

| | |
|---|---|
| Calories | 266 kcal |
| Fat | 16.2 g |
| Carbohydrates | 3.7g |
| Protein | 25.3 g |
| Cholesterol | 124 mg |
| Sodium | 586 mg |

## Ingredients

1 cup egg substitute
1 egg
3 green onions, thinly sliced
8 pepperoni slices, diced
1/2 tsp garlic powder

1 tsp melted butter
1/4 cup grated Romano cheese
1 pinch salt and ground black pepper to taste

## Directions

1. Get a bowl, evenly mix the following in order: garlic powder, egg substitute, pepperoni, green onions, and egg.
2. Fry your eggs in melted butter in a covered frying pan with low heat for 14 mins.
3. Before serving garnish with Romano cheese and pepper and salt.
4. Enjoy.

# MACARONI
# and Eggs

Prep Time: 10 mins
Total Time: 25 mins

Servings per Recipe: 4
| | |
|---|---|
| Calories | 243 kcal |
| Fat | 8.5 g |
| Carbohydrates | 29.9 g |
| Protein | 11.5 g |
| Cholesterol | 194 mg |
| Sodium | 93 mg |

## Ingredients

1 1/2 cups elbow macaroni
1 tbsp butter
1/4 tsp paprika (optional)
salt and ground black pepper to taste

4 large eggs, lightly beaten

## Directions

1. Boil macaroni in salt and water for 9 mins until al dente.
2. Get a frying pan and melt some butter in it. Then add in your pasta to the melted butter along with some: pepper, paprika, and salt.
3. Add eggs to the pasta and do not stir anything for 2 mins. Then for 6 mins continue cooking the eggs but now you can stir. Turn off the heat.
4. Place a lid on the pan and let the eggs continue to cook without heat.

# *Florentine* Style

🥣 Prep Time: 10 mins
🕐 Total Time: 20 mins

Servings per Recipe: 3
| | |
|---|---|
| Calories | 279 kcal |
| Fat | 22.9 g |
| Carbohydrates | 4.1g |
| Protein | 15.7 g |
| Cholesterol | 408 mg |
| Sodium | 276 mg |

## Ingredients

2 tbsps butter
1/2 cup mushrooms, sliced
2 cloves garlic, minced
1/2 (10 oz.) package fresh spinach
6 large eggs, slightly beaten

salt and ground black pepper to taste
3 tbsps cream cheese, cut into small pieces

## Directions

1. Fry your garlic and mushrooms in melted butter in a frying pan for 2 mins. Then mix in your spinach and cook this for another 4 mins.
2. Finally add some pepper and salt and your eggs to the mix and let the eggs set completely. Once the eggs have set you want to flip them.
3. Add a bit of cream cheese to the eggs and let it cook for about 4 mins.

# SCRAMBLED EGGS
# Done Right

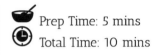

Prep Time: 5 mins
Total Time: 10 mins

Servings per Recipe: 1

| | |
|---|---|
| Calories | 420 kcal |
| Fat | 33.1 g |
| Carbohydrates | 9.7g |
| Protein | 23.1 g |
| Cholesterol | 575 mg |
| Sodium | 755 mg |

## Ingredients

3 large eggs
1 pinch red pepper flakes
9 cherry tomatoes, halved
2 tbsps crumbled feta cheese
1 tbsp very thinly sliced fresh basil
leaves

olive oil
1 pinch sea salt

## Directions

1.  Get a bowl and evenly mix the following: basil, eggs, feta, red pepper flakes, and tomatoes.
2.  Fry in hot olive oil for a few secs without any stirring so the eggs set. Then begin to scramble them for 1 min.
3.  Ideally you want your eggs to be only lightly set. Remove them from the heat. Season with salt.
4.  Enjoy.

# *Chipotle*
# Bacon and Eggs

Prep Time: 10 mins
Total Time: 30 mins

Servings per Recipe: 4
| | |
|---|---|
| Calories | 381 kcal |
| Fat | 29.6 g |
| Carbohydrates | 12.2g |
| Protein | 20.5 g |
| Cholesterol | 310 mg |
| Sodium | 553 mg |

## Ingredients

4 slices bacon, chopped
6 eggs
2 tbsps sour cream
1 tbsp oil, or as needed
1 tbsp chipotle-flavored hot sauce (such as Tabasco(R) Chipotle Pepper Sauce)

3 vine-ripened tomatoes, chopped
1 avocado - peeled, pitted, and chopped
1 (6 oz.) package fresh spinach
1/2 cup shredded Cheddar cheese
salt and ground black pepper to taste

## Directions

1. Get a bowl, evenly mix: sour cream and eggs.
2. Fry your bacon for 11 mins. Then remove oil excess with some paper towels.
3. Now you want to cook your eggs in oil in a frying pan for 7 minutes with your hot sauce.
4. Add in your spinach, avocadoes and tomatoes and cook for 1 more min.
5. Finally top everything with cheddar and a bit more pepper and salt. Let the cheese melt with another .5 to 1 min of cooking time.

# BREAKFAST EGGS
# from India

Prep Time: 5 mins

Total Time: 15 mins

Servings per Recipe: 2
| | |
|---|---|
| Calories | 367 kcal |
| Fat | 32.9 g |
| Carbohydrates | 12.4g |
| Protein | 8.4 g |
| Cholesterol | 186 mg |
| Sodium | 157 mg |

## Ingredients

1/4 cup vegetable oil
1 tsp garam masala
1 tsp ground turmeric
1 tsp ground coriander
salt to taste
1/2 cup finely chopped onion

3 green chili peppers, sliced
2 large eggs

## Directions

1. Get a bowl and add your eggs to it. Then whisk them.
2. In a frying pan, cook the following in hot oil for 6 mins: salt, green chili peppers, garam masala, onions, coriander, and turmeric.
3. After 6 mins pour in your eggs to the seasoned onions and chilies and scramble for 5 mins.

20

Breakfast Eggs from India

# Fried Eggs
# and Shrimp

🥣 Prep Time: 10 mins
🕐 Total Time: 25 mins

Servings per Recipe: 3
| | |
|---|---|
| Calories | 236 kcal |
| Fat | 14.9 g |
| Carbohydrates | 8.8g |
| Protein | 16.8 g |
| Cholesterol | 404 mg |
| Sodium | 1237 mg |

## Ingredients

1 tbsp vegetable oil, or as needed
1 onion, chopped
6 eggs, beaten
1 tsp salt
10 cooked large shrimp

1/4 cup cocktail sauce

## Directions

1. Fry onions in hot oil for 11 mins. Then mix in the eggs and salt. Continue frying for 6 mins.

2. Add in your shrimp and cocktail sauce and continue to cook for 5 more mins.

3. Enjoy.

# MAGGIE'S
# Favorite Eggs

Prep Time: 15 mins
Total Time: 55 mins

Servings per Recipe: 8

| | |
|---|---|
| Calories | 492 kcal |
| Fat | 38.2 g |
| Carbohydrates | 12.8g |
| Protein | 27 g |
| Cholesterol | 343 mg |
| Sodium | 1683 mg |

## Ingredients

1 (1 lb) bulk pork sausage
12 eggs, beaten
1/3 cup sour cream
1 (7 oz.) can chopped green chilies
1 (24 oz.) jar salsa
1 cup shredded Cheddar cheese

1 cup shredded Monterey Jack cheese
1/2 cup pickled jalapeno pepper slices, or to taste
2 avocados, sliced

## Directions

1. Coat a baking dish with oil or nonstick spray and set your oven to 350 degrees before doing anything else.
2. Get a bowl and whisk all your eggs together in it. Enter the eggs into the greased dish. And bake it in the oven for 15 mins.
3. For 8 mins fry your sausage in hot oil and then crumble.
4. After eggs have baked for 15 mins remove them from the oven layer your sausage, jalapeno, salsa, green chilies, Monterey, and cheddar over the eggs.
5. Put everything back in the oven for 23 mins.
6. Enjoy. With a topping of avocado.

# Egg
# Salad

Prep Time: 10 mins
Total Time: 10 mins

Servings per Recipe: 8

| | |
|---|---|
| Calories | 83 kcal |
| Fat | 5.3 g |
| Carbohydrates | 1.3g |
| Protein | 6.8 g |
| Cholesterol | 212 mg |
| Sodium | 141 mg |

## Ingredients

8 hard-cooked eggs, chopped
1/4 cup plain fat-free yogurt
1 tbsp parsley flakes
1/4 tsp onion powder

1/4 tsp paprika
1/4 tsp salt

## Directions

1. To make this salad get a bowl: and combine all the ingredients until completely smooth and even.
2. Enjoy with toasted bread.

# EASY
# Spicy Eggs

Prep Time: 10 mins
Total Time: 10 mins

Servings per Recipe: 4
| | |
|---|---|
| Calories | 46 kcal |
| Fat | 3.4 g |
| Carbohydrates | 0.4g |
| Protein | 3.3 g |
| Cholesterol | 108 mg |
| Sodium | 33 mg |

## Ingredients

2 hard-cooked eggs, cut in half
lengthwise
1 tbsp cream-style horseradish sauce

## Directions

1. Take your eggs and take out the yolks. Put the yolks aside in a bowl.
2. Add horseradish to the yolks and mix everything evenly.
3. Simply fill each egg white with the yolk mix and chill before serving them.

# Buttery Eggs

 Prep Time: 10 mins
Total Time: 20 mins

| Servings per Recipe | 34 |
| --- | --- |
| Calories | 311 kcal |
| Fat | 20.9 g |
| Carbohydrates | 12.4g |
| Protein | 18.6 g |
| Cholesterol | 405 mg |
| Sodium | 261 mg |

## Ingredients

6 eggs
2 tbsps butter
2 tbsps all-purpose flour
2 cups milk

1/8 tsp ground white pepper, if desired
salt and pepper to taste

## Directions

1. Get a big saucepan and fill it with water. Add your eggs to the water and bring it to a rolling boil. Once boiling for about a minute then remove the pan from the heat and place a lid on it. Let it stand for about 13 mins.
2. After 13 mins take out the eggs, remove the shells, and dice them.
3. Now drain the saucepan of its water and melt some butter in it. Once the butter is melted add some flour and heat it until a ball-like shape begins to form. Then add in your milk and lightly stir until the sauce begins to boil.
4. While boiling add in: salt, white pepper, chopped eggs, and black pepper. Heat everything up then remove it all from the heat.
5. Enjoy with your favorite toasted bread.

# BREAKFAST
# In Texas

Prep Time: 30 mins
Total Time: 55 mins

Servings per Recipe: 6
| | |
|---|---|
| Calories | 799 kcal |
| Fat | 58.3 g |
| Carbohydrates | 30.8g |
| Protein | 36.8 g |
| Cholesterol | 392 mg |
| Sodium | 2120 mg |

## Ingredients

1 lb sausage
9 slices white bread, cut into cubes
9 eggs, beaten
1 (11 oz.) can condensed cream of
Cheddar cheese soup
3 cups milk

1 1/2 tsps salt
8 oz. shredded Cheddar cheese

## Directions

1. Before doing anything else grease a baking dish some butter.
2. Get a frying pan and stir fry your sausage and then crumble it. Cook until it is fully done. Remove oil excess.
3. Get a bowl combine evenly: salt, eggs, milk, and soup.
4. Enter into your baking dish the cubed bread, and sausage.
5. Pour the wet mix over the bread cubes in the baking dish. Then top everything with cheese.
6. Cover the dish with foil and put it in the frig throughout the night.
7. Once 8 hours has elapsed you want to set the oven to 350 degrees. Once the oven is hot bake the casserole for at least an hour.
8. Enjoy.

# *Eggs* from Ireland

Prep Time: 15 mins
Total Time: 35 mins

Servings per Recipe: 4
| | |
|---|---|
| Calories | 425 kcal |
| Fat | 13.6 g |
| Carbohydrates | 62.6g |
| Protein | 15.1 g |
| Cholesterol | 294 mg |
| Sodium | 297 mg |

## Ingredients

2 tbsps butter
6 potatoes, peeled and sliced
1 onion, minced
1 green bell pepper, chopped

6 eggs, beaten

## Directions

1.  In hot oil and in a frying pan cook your onions, potatoes, and peppers until the potatoes are fully browned.
2.  Simple add your eggs to the potatoes and continue frying until the eggs are firm.
3.  Enjoy.

# EGGS
# from Mexico

 Prep Time: 30 mins

Total Time: 55 mins

Servings per Recipe: 12

| | |
|---|---|
| Calories | 541 kcal |
| Fat | 42.3 g |
| Carbohydrates | 15.7g |
| Protein | 24.8 g |
| Cholesterol | 98 mg |
| Sodium | 1390 mg |

## Ingredients

24 jalapeno peppers
1 lb sausage
2 cups all-purpose baking mix
1 (16 oz.) package Cheddar cheese,
shredded
1 tbsp crushed red pepper flakes

1 tbsp garlic salt
1 (16 oz.) package Monterey Jack cheese,
cubed

## Directions

1. Coat a casserole dish with nonstick spray and then set your oven to 325 degrees before doing anything else.
2. Get a bowl, evenly mix: garlic salt, sausage, red pepper flakes, cheddar, and baking mix. Set aside.
3. Take out the pulp and seeds in all the jalapenos by cutting an incision into each one and using your fingers to remove the insides.
4. Fill the peppers with the Monterey cubes. Cover each pepper with the sausage mix in your bowl and try to shape everything into balls.
5. Enter everything into the casserole dish and cook in the oven for 25 to 30 mins.
6. Enjoy.

# *Eggs*
# from Italy

🥣 Prep Time: 5 mins
🕐 Total Time: 15 mins

Servings per Recipe: 4
| | |
|---|---|
| Calories | 154 kcal |
| Fat | 11.9 g |
| Carbohydrates | 5.3g |
| Protein | 7.5 g |
| Cholesterol | 186 mg |
| Sodium | 374 mg |

## Ingredients

2 tbsps extra virgin olive oil
4 ripe tomatoes, chopped
4 eggs

salt and pepper to taste

## Directions

1. For 6 mins cook your tomatoes in hot oil. Simply break the eggs into the tomatoes and add some pepper and salt. Fry until you reach the firmness that you enjoy the most.

# MAYO,
# Mustard and Eggs

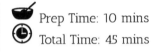 Prep Time: 10 mins

Total Time: 45 mins

Servings per Recipe: 12

| | |
|---|---|
| Calories | 57 kcal |
| Fat | 4.6 g |
| Carbohydrates | 0.8g |
| Protein | 3.3 g |
| Cholesterol | 93 mg |
| Sodium | 158 mg |

## Ingredients

6 eggs
2 tbsps mayonnaise
1 tbsp spicy brown mustard (such as Gulden's(R))
1 tsp hot mustard (such as Sweet Hot Mister Mustard(R))

1 tsp white sugar
salt and pepper to taste
paprika for garnish (optional)
6 pimento-stuffed green olives, cut in half

## Directions

1.  Get a saucepan and enter your eggs into the pan.
2.  Fill the pan with water so that it is 1 inch higher than the eggs. Bring the water to a rolling boil. Turn off the heat. Place a lid on the pan. And let the eggs sit in the water for 16 mins. Remove all the liquid.
3.  Remove the shells from the eggs and cut them in half. Put all of the egg yolks in a separate container.
4.  Add to the yolks the following: pepper, mayo, salt, spicy brown mustard, sugar, and hot mustard. Mash everything together.
5.  Fill each egg half with the yolk mix. Then garnish with some fresh paprika.
6.  Enjoy.

# Vegetarian
# Eggs

 Prep Time: 10 mins

Total Time: 25 mins

Servings per Recipe: 6
| | |
|---|---|
| Calories | 182 kcal |
| Fat | 15.8 g |
| Carbohydrates | 2.4g |
| Protein | 8.1 g |
| Cholesterol | 192 mg |
| Sodium | 159 mg |

## Ingredients

1/4 cup olive oil
1/4 cup sliced fresh mushrooms
1/4 cup chopped onions
1/4 cup chopped green bell peppers
6 eggs

1/4 cup milk
1/4 cup chopped fresh tomato
1/4 cup shredded Cheddar cheese

## Directions

1. Get a bowl mix: milk, eggs, and veggies with tomatoes.
2. Fry onions, mushrooms, and peppers until the onion are see-through in hot olive oil in a frying pan.
3. Then pour in eggs and veggies continue cooking until the eggs are firm.
4. Right before everything is finished top the eggs with your cheese and cook for another minute.
5. Enjoy.

# PROSCIUTTO
# Eggs

Prep Time: 15 mins
Total Time: 40 mins

Servings per Recipe: 4

| | |
|---|---|
| Calories | 199 kcal |
| Fat | 15.7 g |
| Carbohydrates | 5.1g |
| Protein | 10.8 g |
| Cholesterol | 175 mg |
| Sodium | 446 mg |

## Ingredients

1 bunch fresh asparagus, trimmed
1 tbsp extra-virgin olive oil
1 tbsp olive oil
2 oz. minced prosciutto
ground black pepper
1 tsp distilled white vinegar

1 pinch salt
4 eggs
1/2 lemon, zested and juiced
1 pinch ground black pepper

## Directions

1. Set your oven to 425 degree before doing anything else.
2. Get a casserole dish and enter into it your asparagus and coat the veggies with some olive oil.
3. Stir fry your prosciutto and some black pepper for 5 mins in 1 tbsp of olive oil.
4. Layer the meat over the asparagus. Bake for 10 mins.
5. Then toss the contents and bake for 6 more mins.
6. Boil 3 inches of water and add in some salt and your vinegar.
7. Then break an egg in the water. Continue for all eggs. Let the eggs poach for 6 mins. Then remove them from the water.
8. Now plate your asparagus and coat them with a bit of lemon juice then topped with an egg. Then some zest of lemon and finally a bit of pepper.
9. Enjoy.

# *Autumn*
# Acorn Quiche

🥣 Prep Time: 15 mins
🕐 Total Time: 1 hr 30 mins

Servings per Recipe: 6
| | |
|---|---|
| Calories | 165 kcal |
| Carbohydrates | 20 g |
| Cholesterol | 142 mg |
| Fat | 4.8 g |
| Protein | 12.6 g |
| Sodium | 69 mg |

## Ingredients

2 acorn squash
1 red onion, chopped
1 cup chopped cooked turkey
4 eggs

1 tbsp pumpkin pie spice
salt to taste

## Directions

1. Preheat your oven at 350 degrees F and put some oil over the quiche dish.
2. Put squash into a baking dish and then bake it in the preheated oven for one full hour before cutting this in half, removing seeds and scrapping the meat out in a bowl.
3. Combine squash, turkey, eggs, pumpkin pie spice, onion and salt together in a medium sized bowl before pouring this mixture into the quiche dish
4. Bake in the preheated oven for about 45 minutes or until the top of the quiche is golden brown in color.

# HOW TO
# Boil an Egg

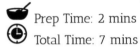 Prep Time: 2 mins

Total Time: 7 mins

Servings per Recipe: 2

| | |
|---|---|
| Calories | 143.0 |
| Fat | 9.5g |
| Cholesterol | 372.0mg |
| Sodium | 1326.0mg |
| Carbohydrates | 0.7g |
| Protein | 12.5g |

## Ingredients

4 large eggs
1 tsp. salt
6 cups water

## Directions

1. Place the 6 cups of water in a saucepan and allow to boil.
2. Stir in salt and allow to boil.
3. With the use of an egg pricker or a fork to pierce the end of the egg.
4. Insert into boiling water and boil for 6 minutes.
5. Dip in cold water, break it and serve.
6. Enjoy.

# How to
# Pickle an Egg

Prep Time: 20 mins
Total Time: 35 mins

Servings per Recipe: 12
| | |
|---|---|
| Calories | 120.5 |
| Fat | 5.3g |
| Cholesterol | 186.5mg |
| Sodium | 258.1mg |
| Carbohydrates | 7.8g |
| Protein | 6.4g |

## Ingredients

12 hard-boiled eggs, peeled
1 large empty sterilized glass jar
4 cups vinegar
1 tsp. salt

2 medium onions, chopped
1/3 cup sugar
1 tbsp. pickling spices

## Directions

1. Place the peeled eggs in a bowl.
2. Put the rest of the ingredients into a saucepan and allow to boil for 6 minutes.
3. Empty the mixture over the eggs in the bowl.
4. Cover with wrap and leave overnight.
5. Can be kept in the refrigerator for many weeks.
6. Enjoy.

# CRACKED
# Tomato Baguettes

 Prep Time: 15 mins

Total Time: 15 mins

Servings per Recipe: 1
| | |
|---|---|
| Calories | 186.1 |
| Fat. | 5.5g |
| Cholesterol | 186.0mg |
| Sodium | 241.3mg |
| Carbohydrates | 23.2g |
| Protein | 11.1g |

## Ingredients

1 piece baguette, about 6-inch in length
1 tbsp. mayonnaise
cracked black pepper,

1 medium tomatoes, sliced
1-2 egg, hard-boiled and sliced

## Directions

1. Cut the baguette along the length.
2. Rub with mayonnaise and sprinkle pepper on top.
3. Place a layer of tomato followed by a layer of eggs on top.
4. Place the top part of the baguette.
5. Enjoy.

# 6-Minute
# Poached Eggs

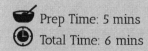 Prep Time: 5 mins

Total Time: 6 mins

Servings per Recipe: 1

| | |
|---|---|
| Calories | 71.6 |
| Fat | 4.7g |
| Cholesterol | 186.0mg |
| Sodium | 73.4mg |
| Carbohydrates | 0.3g |
| Protein | 6.2g |

## Ingredients

1 large egg
1/8 tsp. white vinegar
1/3 cup water
salt and pepper

## Directions

1. Pour white vinegar and water into a 6 oz. measuring cup.
2. Crack the egg into the measuring cup. Take a toothpick to burst the egg yolk and use a plastic wrap to cover the dish.
3. Cook for 2 minutes in a Microwave oven until done.
4. Use a large spoon and quickly transfer the egg from water to serving dish.
5. Season with salt and pepper.
6. Enjoy.

# SHAKSHOUKA
# (Levantine Spicy Eggs)

 Prep Time: 20 mins

Total Time: 40 mins

Servings per Recipe: 4
| | |
|---|---|
| Calories | 209 kcal |
| Carbohydrates | 12.9 g |
| Cholesterol | 164 mg |
| Fat | 15 g |
| Protein | 7.8 g |
| Sodium | 654 mg |

## Ingredients

3 tbsps olive oil
1 1/3 cups chopped onion
1 cup thinly sliced bell peppers, any color
2 cloves garlic, minced, or to taste
2 1/2 cups chopped tomatoes
1 tsp ground cumin

1 tsp paprika
1 tsp salt
1 hot chile pepper, seeded and finely chopped, or to taste
4 eggs

## Directions

1. Cook onion, garlic and bell peppers in hot oil for about five minutes or until you see that the vegetables have softened up.
2. Add the mixture of chili pepper, tomatoes, salt, cumin and paprika into this pan before cooking it for another ten minutes.
3. Make space for eggs in the mixture and cook these eggs by covering the pan, and cooking it for five minutes or until the eggs are firm.
4. Serve.

# *College* Breakfast Burritos

Prep Time: 10 mins
Total Time: 10 mins

Servings per Recipe: 1

| | |
|---|---|
| Calories | 358.4 |
| Fat | 21.2g |
| Cholesterol | 401.6mg |
| Sodium | 638.3mg |
| Carbohydrates | 18.4g |
| Protein | 22.0g |

## Ingredients

2 eggs
salt and pepper
1 flour tortilla
1/4 cup shredded cheddar cheese

1 tbsp. taco sauce

## Directions

1. Add salt, pepper and a bit of water into the eggs and beat well.
2. Spray a skillet with a non-stick cooking spray.
3. Fold in the eggs to the skillet and allow to scramble.
4. Heat the flour tortilla on a stovetop for 2 seconds per side.
5. Spread the eggs in the middle of the tortilla and sprinkle taco sauce and cheese on top
6. Roll up and serve.
7. Enjoy.

# MESA
# Deviled Eggs

 Prep Time: 15 mins

Total Time: 35 mins

Servings per Recipe: 6

| | |
|---|---|
| Calories | 81.3 |
| Fat | 5.3g |
| Cholesterol | 186.5mg |
| Sodium | 261.1mg |
| Carbohydrates | 1.3g |
| Protein | 6.4g |

## Ingredients

6 large hard-boiled eggs
salt and black pepper
2 tbsps. real mayonnaise
1 tsp. prepared yellow mustard

2 diced gherkins
1 sliced jalapeno
paprika

## Directions

1. Cool the eggs and remove the shells; cut into halves.
2. Separate the egg yolks from egg whites into a bowl.
3. With the use of a fork pound the yolk until partially smooth.
4. Stir in 2 tbsps. of Mayonnaise, gherkins, mustard, salt and jalapeno and combine well.
5. Place the mixture into a sealable bag, secure the seal and nip off a corner of the sealable bag.
6. Pour the mixture through the corner of the bag into egg whites.
7. Sprinkle paprika on top of the egg whites.
8. Refrigerate for 2 to 2 1/2 hours until chilled prior to serving.
9. Enjoy.

# *Easier*
# Egg Foo Yung

Prep Time: 5 mins
Total Time: 12 mins

Servings per Recipe: 1

| | |
|---|---|
| Calories | 851.7 |
| Fat | 59.6g |
| Cholesterol | 463.5mg |
| Sodium | 2531.6mg |
| Carbohydrates | 57.6g |
| Protein | 22.7g |

## Ingredients

1 (3 ounce) packages ramen noodles
3 tbsps. butter, divided
2 large eggs
2 green onions, chopped

1/2 tsp. sesame oil
1/2 tsp. soy sauce
1/2 tsp. baking powder

## Directions

1. Follow the package instructions to cook the noodles. Remove excess water with the use of a colander.
2. In a bowl beat the eggs, seasoning, onions, soy sauce, sesame oil and baking powder with the use of a fork. Stir in the noodles.
3. In a frying pan heat the butter.
4. Place the noodle mixture in the frying pan.
5. Continuously turn the noodles with a spatula for about 3 minutes, until egg is done
6. Turn again and leave for 2 minutes.
7. Can be eaten with egg foo yung sauce or soy sauce.
8. Enjoy.

# HOW TO
# Make Egg Noodles

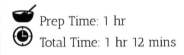

Prep Time: 1 hr
Total Time: 1 hr 12 mins

Servings per Recipe: 10

| | |
|---|---|
| Calories | 112.9 |
| Fat | 1.9g |
| Cholesterol | 68.4mg |
| Sodium | 475.0mg |
| Carbohydrates | 19.2g |
| Protein | 3.9g |

## Ingredients

2 cups flour
3 egg yolks
1 egg

2 tsps. salt
1/4-1/2 cup water

## Directions

1. In a bowl, place the flour and make a dent in the middle. Add the egg, egg yolks and salt.
2. Combine the mixture thoroughly with the use of your hands.
3. Add 1 tbsp of water at a time and combine well.
4. Flour a wooden board and place the dough on it; knead for about 12 minutes, then leave it covered for 10 minutes
5. Separate the dough into four portions.
6. Roll the dough on the floured wooden board into thin rectangles, keep the balance dough covered with a wet cloth.
7. Slice the dough into 1/8" cross wise strips.
8. Pat dry with a towel for about 2-3 hours.
9. Once dry break into strips.
10. Add 1 tbsp salt to 3 quarts of boiling water and cook for 13-16 minutes until done.
11. Drain the excess water using a colander.
12. Enjoy.

# *Easiest*
# Scotch Eggs

Prep Time: 1 hr 30 mins
Total Time: 2 hrs

Servings per Recipe: 4
Calories           602.9
Fat                32.9g
Cholesterol        314.2mg
Sodium             838.5mg
Carbohydrates      39.6g
Protein            34.2g

## Ingredients

1 lb. ground lean turkey
1/2 tsp. salt
1 tsp. rubbed sage
1/2 tsp. pepper
1/2 tsp. thyme
1/8 tsp. clove

4 large eggs, hard boiled
flour
1 large egg
2 cups dry breadcrumbs

## Directions

1. Combine the turkey with salt, sage, pepper, thyme and cloves and separate into 4 similar quantities.

2. Hard boil the eggs for 10 minutes.

3. Peel the eggs and put them in cold water. Then coat the peeled eggs in flour.

4. Cover each egg entirely with a part of meat.

5. Whisk the kept aside large egg.

6. Insert each egg in the whisked egg and season with fine dry bread crumbs.

7. Leave in the refrigerator for about 1 hour.

8. Cook on a parchment sheet in the oven at a temperature of 400F for 35 minutes until golden brown in color.

9. Enjoy.

# TAIWANESE STYLE
# Egg Drop Soup

 Prep Time: 5 mins

Total Time: 15 mins

Servings per Recipe: 2

| | |
|---|---|
| Calories | 111.9 |
| Fat | 4.4g |
| Cholesterol | 93.0mg |
| Sodium | 1738.8mg |
| Carbohydrates | 5.7g |
| Protein | 10.6g |

## Ingredients

3 cups chicken broth
1/2 tsp. salt
2 tbsps. cold water
1 tbsp. cornstarch

1 egg
1 scallion, with tops, chopped

## Directions

1. Pour the chicken broth into a saucepan and allow to boil.
2. Stir in 1/2 tsp salt and combine well.
3. In a bowl, mix the cornstarch and water; add to the broth in the saucepan.
4. Whisk the egg and add a little of the broth. Stir in the mixture to the broth and continue to stir all along. Cook until the mixture becomes thick.
5. Serve garnished with scallion.
6. Enjoy.

# *Deep* Egg Salad Sandwiches

🍲 Prep Time: 10 mins
🕐 Total Time: 20 mins

Servings per Recipe: 8
| | |
|---|---|
| Calories | 298.7 |
| Fat | 15.2g |
| Cholesterol | 158.9mg |
| Sodium | 761.3mg |
| Carbohydrates | 31.3g |
| Protein | 8.8g |

## Ingredients

6 eggs, hard cooked, cooled and diced
1/4 cup butter, melted
1/2 cup Miracle Whip
1/4 tsp. salt
1/4 tsp. Lawry's Seasoned Salt
1/8 tsp. garlic salt
1/8 tsp. celery salt
1/4 tsp. dill weed

16 slices bread
Additional:
2 tbsps. onions, chopped
1/2 cup celery, chopped
1/4 cup pickle relish
1/2 cup green olives

## Directions

1. Combine the eggs, miracle whip, butter and seasonings.
2. Keep the mixture refrigerated until ready to use.
3. Apply the spread on one slice of bread and place another slice on top.
4. Add the other ingredients as desired.
5. Enjoy.

# HARD BOILED
# for the Party

Prep Time: 5 mins
Total Time: 15 mins

Servings per Recipe: 12
Calories           71.5
Fat                4.7g
Cholesterol        186.0mg
Sodium             71.0mg
Carbohydrates      0.3g
Protein            6.2g

## Ingredients

12 eggs
water

## Directions

1. Insert the 12 eggs into a saucepan and cover with water up to about 1".
2. Cover with lid and allow to boil
3. Transfer from heat. Keep aside to cool for about 12 minutes.
4. Wash off with cold water and dip in ice water for a few minutes.
5. Enjoy.

# *How to*
# Make a Custard Pie

Prep Time: 20 mins
Total Time: 55 mins

Servings per Recipe: 8
| | |
|---|---|
| Calories | 263.6 |
| Fat | 11.7g |
| Cholesterol | 77.3mg |
| Sodium | 256.0mg |
| Carbohydrates | 32.9g |
| Protein | 6.5g |

## Ingredients

1 (9 inch) unbaked pie shells, deep dish
3 eggs, beaten
3/4 cup white sugar
1/4 tsp. salt
1 tsp. vanilla extract
1 egg white

2 1/2 cups scalded whole milk
1/4 tsp. ground nutmeg
3 drops yellow food coloring

## Directions

1. First set the oven to 400F.
2. Combine the sugar, eggs, vanilla and salt. Stir in the milk. If you require more color stir in a little food coloring.
3. Rub egg white on the sides and bottom of the pie shells. Fold in the custard mixture and sprinkle nutmeg on top.
4. Cook for 42-52 minutes in the oven.
5. Transfer to rack and allow to cool.
6. Enjoy.

# SWEET
# Egg Based Cookies

 Prep Time: 10 mins
Total Time: 20 mins

Servings per Recipe: 60
| | |
|---|---|
| Calories | 70.8 |
| Fat | 3.5g |
| Cholesterol | 24.7mg |
| Sodium | 51.5mg |
| Carbohydrates | 9.0g |
| Protein | 0.8g |

## Ingredients

1 cup butter
1 1/2 cups sugar
6 egg yolks
2 1/2 cups all-purpose flour
1 tsp. baking soda
1 tsp. cream of tartar

1 tsp. vanilla extract
1/2 tsp. lemon extract
1/2 tsp. orange extract
1 pinch salt

## Directions

1. Mix sugar and butter in a bowl and whisk until smooth.
2. In another bowl whisk the egg yolks, salt and extracts.
3. Add the egg mixture to the sugar mixture and combine well.
4. Combine all the dry ingredients in another bowl and mix well.
5. Stir in the dry ingredients mixture into the egg/sugar mixture.
6. Shape the mixture into balls similar to walnuts.
7. Brush the balls with sugar. Grease a cookie sheet, place the balls on the sheet and flatten slightly.
8. Cook in the oven for 12 minutes at 350 degrees F until done.
9. Enjoy.

# Twin City
# Egg Sandwich

🥣 Prep Time: 2 mins
🕐 Total Time: 7 mins

Servings per Recipe: 1
Calories            304.3
Fat                 15.9g
Cholesterol         215.4mg
Sodium              450.8mg
Carbohydrates       21.9g
Protein             17.3g

## Ingredients

1 large egg
salt and pepper
1 slice of processed cheddar cheese
1 hamburger bun
prepared mustard

## Directions

1. Grease a skillet with butter and break the egg into the skillet.
2. Pierce the yolk and allow to cook; turn on to the other side and cook for a few minutes
3. Season with salt and pepper.
4. Remove from heat.
5. Put the cheese slice on top and allow it to melt.
6. Toast the bun using the skillet to your preference.
7. Apply mustard on the bun and lay the egg inside.
8. Serve with salads.
9. Enjoy.

# WESTCOTT
# Pancakes

Prep Time: 5 mins
Total Time: 10 mins

Servings per Recipe: 1
| | |
|---|---|
| Calories | 248.0 |
| Fat | 9.9g |
| Cholesterol | 372.0mg |
| Sodium | 143.1mg |
| Carbohydrates | 27.6g |
| Protein | 13.8g |

## Ingredients

2 eggs
1 banana
cooking spray

## Directions

1. Puree the bananas and beat the eggs into the bananas.
2. Spray oil on a skillet and allow to heat. Fold the batter into the skillet and cook for 32 seconds on each side.
3. Serve with maple syrup.
4. Enjoy.

# 4 Street Park
# Eggs for Easter

Prep Time: 1 hr 30 mins
Total Time: 3 hrs

Servings per Recipe: 1

| | |
|---|---|
| Calories | 373.1 |
| Fat | 19.0g |
| Cholesterol | 22.3mg |
| Sodium | 176.6mg |
| Carbohydrates | 47.4g |
| Protein | 5.5g |

## Ingredients

1/4 lb. butter, softened
8 ounces cream cheese, softened
2 lbs. confectioners' sugar
1 1/2 cups peanut butter
1 1/2 tsps. vanilla

1/2 tsp. salt
20 - 23 ounces milk chocolate chips

## Directions

1. Combine the cream cheese with butter and mix well.
2. Gradually add the sugar and stir well.
3. Stir in vanilla, peanut butter and salt and blend well.
4. Refrigerate the mixture and leave for 60 minutes.
5. Shape the mix into egg shapes and leave in the refrigerator once again for 60 minutes.
6. Place the chocolate in a microwave safe bowl and microwave until melted.
7. Coat the bottom of the eggs in chocolate mixture., then coat the top as well.
8. Spread the eggs on a parchment paper lined pan to set the chocolate.
9. Insert each egg into a paper muffin cup.
10. Sprinkle the eggs with pastel jimmies or Easter sprinkles.
11. Enjoy.

# CHIVE
# Scramble

Prep Time: 5 mins
Total Time: 10 mins

Servings per Recipe: 3

| | |
|---|---|
| Calories | 279.3 |
| Fat | 24.7g |
| Cholesterol | 416.2mg |
| Sodium | 247.1mg |
| Carbohydrates | 1.0g |
| Protein | 12.8g |

## Ingredients

6 large eggs
3 tbsps. butter, diced
2 tbsps. crème fraiche
ground sea salt and pepper

3 chives, snipped
3 slices , rustic bread

## Directions

1. Crack the eggs into a heavy skillet and place on a low heat, add 1 1/2 tbsp of butter. Continuously mix the egg whites with the yolks.
2. Stir in the balance butter.
3. Slightly toast the 3 slices of bread.
4. Stir in the crème fraiche to the eggs and lastly add the chives
5. Spread the scrambled eggs on the toast and serve.
6. Enjoy.

# Vegetarian
# Egg Salad

🥄 Prep Time: 10 mins
🕐 Total Time: 10 mins

Servings per Recipe: 4
| | |
|---|---|
| Calories | 371.0 |
| Fat | 31.8g |
| Cholesterol | 10.4mg |
| Sodium | 314.5mg |
| Carbohydrates | 6.7g |
| Protein | 19.7g |

## Ingredients

2 lbs. firm tofu
1/2 cup soy mayonnaise
3 tbsps. Dijon mustard
1 tsp. cayenne pepper
1/2 tsp. turmeric

2 tbsps. chopped parsley
1 tbsp. chopped dill
1/2 cup green onion, diced
salt and pepper

## Directions

1. Drain the firm tofu.
2. Slice the tofu into quarters, use paper towels to wrap the tofu.
3. Leave in the refrigerator for 25 minutes.
4. In a bowl puree the tofu using a wooden spatula.
5. Combine the tofu with the rest of the ingredients.
6. Serve chilled.
7. Enjoy.

# 4-INGREDIENT
# American Fried Rice

 Prep Time: 2 mins

Total Time: 7 mins

Servings per Recipe: 2

| | |
|---|---|
| Calories | 158.1 |
| Fat | 12.8g |
| Cholesterol | 294.2mg |
| Sodium | 157.1mg |
| Carbohydrates | 0.5g |
| Protein | 9.4g |

## Ingredients

rice

1 - 2 tbsp. butter

3 - 4 eggs

salt and pepper

## Directions

1. Place the butter in a frying pan and allow to melt.
2. Stir in the rice and allow to heat.
3. Combine the rice with the butter.
4. In a bowl beat the eggs and fold into the frying pan.
5. Scramble the eggs.
6. Enjoy.

# *Eggs*
# in a Boat I

Prep Time: 1 min

Total Time: 4 mins

Servings per Recipe: 1

| | |
|---|---|
| Calories | 0.0 |
| Fat | 0.0g |
| Cholesterol | 0.0mg |
| Sodium | 0.0mg |
| Carbohydrates | 0.0g |
| Protein | 0.0g |

## Ingredients

egg
bread
butter

salt and pepper

## Directions

1. With the use of a drinking glass cut a round in the middle of the slice of bread.
2. Spray a Nonstick cooking spray on a frying pan and allow to heat.
3. Lay the slice of bread in the frying pan.
4. Place 1/2 tsp. of butter in the center.
5. Break an egg into the middle of the bread with the hole.
6. Once the egg is set, flip the slice of bread onto the other side ensuring not to damage the yolk.
7. Add seasonings.
8. Enjoy.

# ANA'S
# Mozzarella Soufflés

Prep Time: 10 mins
Total Time: 40 mins

Servings per Recipe: 3
| | |
|---|---|
| Calories | 160.3 |
| Fat | 10.5g |
| Cholesterol | 375.7mg |
| Sodium | 155.2mg |
| Carbohydrates | 1.9g |
| Protein | 13.4g |

## Ingredients

6 eggs
1/3 cup milk
garlic salt

ground black pepper
mozzarella cheese, shredded

## Directions

1. Place eggs, garlic salt, milk and pepper in a bowl and leave aside.
2. Take three ramekins and spray with a cooking spray. Stuff the ramekins half full with the mozzarella cheese. Fold in the egg mix into the ramekins.
3. Lay the ramekins on a parchment sheet and leave in the oven for 35 minutes at a temperature of 375F.
4. Serve warm.
5. Enjoy.

# 5th Grader's
# Lunch Sandwich

Prep Time: 5 mins
Total Time: 5 mins

Servings per Recipe: 1

| | |
|---|---|
| Calories | 317.6 |
| Fat | 17.4g |
| Cholesterol | 198.3mg |
| Sodium | 685.4mg |
| Carbohydrates | 27.2g |
| Protein | 12.1g |

## Ingredients

1 egg
2 tsps. margarine
2 slices bread
1 tbsp. Cheez Whiz

salt and pepper
red pepper flakes

## Directions

1. Add margarine or butter into a skillet and heat until melted.
2. Stir in the egg without breaking the yolk and allow to fry for a few minutes.
3. Sprinkle black pepper, salt and pepper flakes on top of the egg.
4. Turn the egg onto the other side. Pierce the egg yolk gently with a fork.
5. Add the Cheez Whiz on top of the slice of bread.
6. Place the egg on top of the slice of bread and top the sandwich with the other bread slice.
7. Transfer the egg filled slices into the skillet and toast until golden in color, turn on to the other side and grill for a few minutes.
8. Enjoy.

# GRANDMA'S
# Eggs for February

 Prep Time: 1 hr 30 mins
Total Time: 3 hrs

Servings per Recipe: 28
| | |
|---|---|
| Calories | 358.0 |
| Fat | 17.1g |
| Cholesterol | 17.6mg |
| Sodium | 122.0mg |
| Carbohydrates | 53.7g |
| Protein | 2.1g |

## Ingredients

1/4 lb. butter, softened
8 ounces cream cheese, softened
2 lbs. confectioners' sugar
1/4 tsp. salt
1 1/2 tsps. vanilla

15 ounces flaked coconut
20 -23 ounces semi-sweet chocolate chips
28 -30 unsalted almonds

## Directions

1.  Combine the cream cheese with butter. Microwave for 47 seconds until soft.
2.  Stir in the sugar gradually, vanilla and salt.
3.  Fold in the coconut and combine well.
4.  Leave in the freezer for 25 minutes.
5.  Remove from the freezer and shape similar to eggs.
6.  Lay the eggs on a parchment sheet covered with foil.
7.  Place 2 nuts on each egg and press lightly.
8.  Heat the chocolate in a boiler and allow to melt.
9.  Coat each egg bottom in the chocolate and place on a platter.
10. Rub melted chocolate on top of each egg.
11. Gently ease out the eggs with a sharp blade and place on a parchment sheet lined with foil.
12. Leave in the freezer for the chocolate to harden.
13. Insert the eggs into paper muffin cups.
14. Cover with foil and leave in the refrigerator.
15. Enjoy.

# Egg Salad
# Chicago

Prep Time: 2 hrs
Total Time: 2 hrs

Servings per Recipe: 5
Calories         231.9
Fat              18.3g
Cholesterol      320.2mg
Sodium           256.1mg
Carbohydrates    5.1g
Protein          11.3g

## Ingredients

1 (3 ounce) packages cream cheese, very soft
1/4-1/3 cup mayonnaise
1 tsp. prepared mustard
1 pinch dill
8 hard-boiled eggs, chopped
1 celery rib, diced

2 green onions, chopped
1/3-1/2 cup green pimento stuffed olive
seasoning salt & ground black pepper
Tabasco sauce

## Directions

1. Mix the cream cheese, mayonnaise, mustard and dill in a bowl.
2. Add the chopped hard-boiled eggs, green onion, celery and olives and combine well; adjust seasonings with Tabasco sauce, salt and pepper.
3. Cover with wrap and leave in the refrigerator for 2 hours and 15 minutes.
4. Enjoy.

# CHINESE
# Steamed Eggs

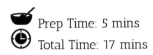

Prep Time: 5 mins
Total Time: 17 mins

Servings per Recipe: 1
| | |
|---|---|
| Calories | 125.8 |
| Fat | 8.3g |
| Cholesterol | 327.3mg |
| Sodium | 124.9mg |
| Carbohydrates | 0.6g |
| Protein | 11.0g |

Ingredients

2 medium eggs
water, for steaming

Directions

1. If the eggs have been kept in the refrigerator take them out and allow them to get into room temperature.
2. Steam the 2 eggs in a steamer on high heat for 14 minutes.
3. Leave for 17 minutes to come to room temperature and rinse with cold water.
4. Peel and serve.
5. Enjoy.

# Pickled
# Egg Salad

Prep Time: 45 mins

Total Time: 55 mins

Servings per Recipe: 4

| | |
|---|---|
| Calories | 268.1 |
| Fat | 12.2g |
| Cholesterol | 312.0mg |
| Sodium | 542.1mg |
| Carbohydrates | 8.4g |
| Protein | 29.6g |

## Ingredients

2 (6 ounce) cans tuna
6 hard-boiled eggs
1/4 cup pickle relish
3/4 cup mayonnaise
1 small onion, chopped

1 tsp. garlic powder
1/2 tsp. salt
1/2 tsp. dill weed

## Directions

1. Smash the eggs with a fork.
2. Mix all the ingredients in a bowl and combine well.
3. Leave in the refrigerator.
4. Serve with crackers.
5. Enjoy.

# FRESNO
# Scramble

Prep Time: 10 mins
Total Time: 20 mins

Servings per Recipe: 2
| | |
|---|---|
| Calories | 262.0 |
| Fat | 22.3g |
| Cholesterol | 97.0mg |
| Sodium | 143.4mg |
| Carbohydrates | 13.5g |
| Protein | 5.5g |

## Ingredients

1 ripe avocado
1 hard-boiled egg
2 tbsps. mayonnaise
1 tsp. garlic powder
salt and pepper

paprika
parsley
1/8 tsp. lemon juice

## Directions

1. Slice the ripe avocado into pieces.
2. Chop the hardboiled egg and combine with avocado.
3. Stir in the balance ingredients.
4. Leave in the refrigerator for a few minutes.
5. Serve with salads.
6. Sprinkle paprika on top of the salad.
7. Enjoy.

# *Butter*
# Baked Scrambled Breakfast

Prep Time: 10 mins
Total Time: 30 mins

Servings per Recipe: 6
Calories                243.3
Fat                     19.0g
Cholesterol             399.4mg
Sodium                  622.0mg
Carbohydrates           3.0g
Protein                 14.3g

## Ingredients

1/4 cup melted butter
12 eggs
1 tsp. salt

1 1/4 cups milk

## Directions

1. First set the oven to 350F.
2. Melt the butter and pour into a casserole dish.
3. Add salt to the eggs and whisk well in a bowl.
4. Stir in the milk.
5. Fold in the mixture to the casserole dish. Leave in the oven without a cover for 12 minutes.
6. Remove from the oven, stir then cook for a further 17 minutes until eggs are done.
7. Enjoy.

# DIJON
# Crème Scramble

Prep Time: 5 mins
Total Time: 10 mins

Servings per Recipe: 6

| | |
|---|---|
| Calories | 217.7 |
| Fat | 16.4g |
| Cholesterol | 392.4mg |
| Sodium | 626.0mg |
| Carbohydrates | 3.7g |
| Protein | 13.5g |

## Ingredients

12 large eggs
3 tbsps. herbs, chopped
1 tsp. salt
1/2 tsp. ground black pepper
3 tbsps. crème fraiche

2 tbsps. Dijon mustard
2 tbsps. butter
3 tomatoes, peeled, seeded, diced, and drained

## Directions

1.  Crack the 12 eggs into a bowl; keep aside two yolks in another bowl. Stir in the salt, pepper and herbs into the first bowl.
2.  Mix the crème fraiche and mustard to the two egg yolks.
3.  Add the butter into a frying pan and allow to melt. Stir in the eggs in the first bowl and cook until creamy and thick in consistency.
4.  Stir in the tomatoes and egg yolk mixture into the frying pan and combine well. Transfer from the heat.
5.  Garnish the eggs with herbs and serve.
6.  Enjoy.

# Creamy
# Baked Eggs

🥣 Prep Time: 10 mins
🕐 Total Time: 1 hr

Servings per Recipe: 12
| | |
|---|---|
| Calories | 207.7 |
| Fat | 12.1g |
| Cholesterol | 178.9mg |
| Sodium | 303.6mg |
| Carbohydrates | 11.6g |
| Protein | 12.6g |

## Ingredients

8 slices bread, cubed
1 cup shredded sharp cheddar cheese
1 cup shredded Monterey jack cheese
10 eggs
2 cups milk
2 tsps. dry mustard
2 tsps. dill
1 tsp. sugar
1 tsp. baking powder
1/2 tsp. white pepper
salt

1/2 small yellow onion, chopped
Additional
chives
green pepper
red pepper
orange bell pepper
yellow bell pepper
mushroom
broccoli

## Directions

1. Grease a baking tray.
2. Lay the cubed slices of bread and sprinkle cheese on top.
3. Whisk the eggs until soft and creamy.
4. Stir in the balance ingredients.
5. Spread the mixture over the bread mixture and leave in the refrigerator for 24 hours.
6. Cook in the oven at a temperature of 350F for 52 minutes until done.
7. Enjoy.

# STOCKHOLM
# Scramble

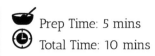

Prep Time: 5 mins
Total Time: 10 mins

Servings per Recipe: 2

| | |
|---|---|
| Calories | 338.6 |
| Fat | 28.9g |
| Cholesterol | 434.4mg |
| Sodium | 324.7mg |
| Carbohydrates | 3.3g |
| Protein | 16.0g |

## Ingredients

4 eggs
4 ounces cream cheese, cut into chunks
1 tbsp. dill, chopped

1 dash garlic powder
salt and pepper

## Directions

1. Whisk the eggs in a bowl.
2. Stir in the pieces of cheese, garlic powder and dill. Adjust seasonings with salt and pepper.
3. Use a cooking spray to spray a frying pan and heat well.
4. Fold in the egg mixture into the frying pan and lower the heat. Continuously scramble until done.
5. Serve warm.
6. Enjoy.

# Mesa Meets Kerala Stuffed Eggs

Prep Time: 10 mins
Total Time: 10 mins

Servings per Recipe: 2
Calories        187.1
Fat             13.2g
Cholesterol     374.9mg
Sodium          204.9mg
Carbohydrates   3.3g
Protein         12.8g

## Ingredients

4 hard-boiled eggs
1 tsp. Dijon mustard
1 tbsp. mayonnaise
1/2 tsp. curry powder

1 pinch cayenne pepper
salt & pepper

## Directions

1. Slice the 4 hardboiled eggs into halves, extract the yolks and insert them into a bowl.
2. Leave aside the whites.
3. Stir in the mayonnaise, mustard, cayenne pepper, salt, pepper and curry powder to the yolks.
4. Spread the yolk mix evenly among the kept aside whites.
5. Cover with a plastic wrap and leave in the refrigerator for 1 or 2 days.
6. Enjoy.

# BUTTERY
# Hard-Boiled Toast

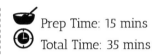 Prep Time: 15 mins

Total Time: 35 mins

| | |
|---|---|
| Servings per Recipe: 2 | |
| Calories | 685.1 |
| Fat | 47.1g |
| Cholesterol | 390.2mg |
| Sodium | 1239.3mg |
| Carbohydrates | 43.3g |
| Protein | 22.2g |

## Ingredients

5 tbsps. butter
4 tbsps. flour
2 cups milk
1/2 tsp. salt
1/4 tsp. white pepper

1/8 tsp. ground nutmeg
3 hard-boiled eggs, chopped
3 - 4 slices bread, to toast
butter

## Directions

1. Heat the butter until melted in a skillet.
2. Fold in the flour.
3. When hot add the milk gradually.
4. Stir in the salt.
5. Beat until bubbly and thick in consistency.
6. Transfer from heat and add the chopped hard-boiled eggs.
7. Toast the slices of bread and butter them.
8. Spread the slices of bread on plates and layer the egg mixture on top.
9. Enjoy.

# Birmingham
# Sandwiches

🥣 Prep Time: 1 min

🕐 Total Time: 4 mins

Servings per Recipe: 1
| | |
|---|---|
| Calories | 200.8 |
| Fat | 5.7g |
| Cholesterol | 186.0mg |
| Sodium | 277.3mg |
| Carbohydrates | 25.5g |
| Protein | 11.3g |

## Ingredients

1 English muffin
1 egg
1 slice light cheese
1 strip turkey bacon, cooked

salt and pepper

## Directions

1. Slightly toast the muffin.
2. Add a tbsp. of water and egg into a microwaveable dish of a similar size to the muffin.
3. Whisk the egg and stir in the strip of bacon.
4. Leave in the microwave for 3 minutes until the egg is done.
5. Piece together the muffin and allow to sit for 2 minutes so that the cheese is melted.
6. Enjoy.

# BACKROAD
# Scramble

Prep Time: 5 mins
Total Time: 10 mins

Servings per Recipe: 2
| | |
|---|---|
| Calories | 132.9 |
| Fat | 8.2g |
| Cholesterol | 283.4mg |
| Sodium | 202.0mg |
| Carbohydrates | 1.4g |
| Protein | 12.3g |

## Ingredients

3 eggs
1/4 cup cottage cheese
salt and pepper

butter

## Directions

1. Place the 3 eggs, 1/4 cup of cottage cheese and seasonings in a food processor.
2. Process until smooth in consistency.
3. Melt the butter in a skillet.
4. Fold in the egg mixture into the skillet.
5. Do not stir but allow the eggs to scramble without being dry.
6. Enjoy.

# Maria's
# Versatile Muffins

🥣 Prep Time: 20 mins

🕐 Total Time: 50 mins

Servings per Recipe: 12

| | |
|---|---|
| Calories | 146.1 |
| Fat | 11.7g |
| Cholesterol | 144.8mg |
| Sodium | 278.1mg |
| Carbohydrates | 0.8g |
| Protein | 8.8g |

## Ingredients

8 eggs
1/2 lb. sausage
1 cup cheddar cheese
salt and pepper

Enhancements
bell pepper, mushrooms, onions, spinach

## Directions

1. Brown the meat and discard the excess fat.

2. Whisk the eggs in a bowl.

3. Stir in cheese, optional ingredients, salt and pepper.

4. Grease a muffin pan and pour the mixture until two thirds full.

5. Cook in the oven at a temperature of 350F for 35 minutes until done.

6. Enjoy.

# 4-INGREDIENT
# Eggs Benedict

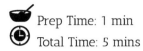 Prep Time: 1 min

Total Time: 5 mins

Servings per Recipe: 1
| | |
|---|---|
| Calories | 222.3 |
| Fat | 14.4g |
| Cholesterol | 558.0mg |
| Sodium | 219.4mg |
| Carbohydrates | 2.8g |
| Protein | 19.4g |

## Ingredients

3 eggs
1 - 3 tbsp. dried dill
salt

pepper

## Directions

1. Fry the eggs or scramble them.
2. Adjust seasonings with salt and pepper.
3. Sprinkle dried dill on top and serve.
4. Enjoy.

# *Artisanal*
# Handmade Pasta

Prep Time: 20 mins
Total Time: 30 mins

Servings per Recipe: 6

| | |
|---|---|
| Calories | 124.3 |
| Fat | 5.8g |
| Cholesterol | 93.0mg |
| Sodium | 329.9mg |
| Carbohydrates | 14.0g |
| Protein | 3.5g |

## Ingredients

1/2 cup tapioca flour
1/2 cup cornstarch
3 tbsps. potato starch
3/4 tsp. salt

4 1/2 tsps. xanthan gum
3 large eggs
1 1/2 tbsps. vegetable oil

## Directions

1. Add flours, xanthan gum and salt into a bowl.
2. Whisk the eggs slightly and stir in the oil.
3. Combine the egg mixture with the flour mixture.
4. Form a dough ball with the mixture and knead for 2 minutes.
5. Dust a breadboard with potato starch and roll to be as lean as possible.
6. Form shapes as required.
7. Slice thin strips for spaghetti and fettuccine.
8. Add salt and 1 tbsp of oil into boiled water and cook the pasta for 14 minutes.
9. Use a colander to drain and rinse with cold water.
10. Enjoy.

# HOUSE
# Fried Rice

Prep Time: 20 mins
Total Time: 30 mins

Servings per Recipe: 4
| | |
|---|---|
| Calories | 516.6 |
| Fat | 7.5g |
| Cholesterol | 240.4mg |
| Sodium | 1247.8mg |
| Carbohydrates | 75.5g |
| Protein | 32.5g |

## Ingredients

12 ounces boneless skinless chicken
breasts
4 eggs
4 dried shiitake mushrooms
1 onion
Sauce:
1/2 cup water

4 tbsps. soy sauce
3 tbsps. mirin
1 tbsp. sugar
5 cups cooked rice
cilantro

## Directions

1. Slice the boneless skinless chicken breasts into lean pieces,
2. Add the mushrooms into mildly hot water and soak until soft. Chop the hard stems and slice into two.
3. Chop the onion into thin pieces.
4. Chop the cilantro into pieces.
5. Combine all the sauce ingredients in a frying pan, cover with lid and allow to boil.
6. Stir in chicken, onion and mushrooms and cook for 5 minutes until the meat is done.
7. Whisk the eggs in a bowl, then fold over the chicken and keep the bowl covered with lid.
8. Leave for 1-2 minutes on a reduced flame until the eggs are firm.
9. Garnish with cilantro.
10. When serving place 1 1/4 cup of rice in a bowl and top up with a layer of about 1/4 of the chicken mixture.
11. Pour the sauce over the ingredients and serve warm.
12. Enjoy.

# Asiago Egg Soufflé

🥣 Prep Time: 20 mins
🕐 Total Time: 45 mins

Servings per Recipe: 4
| | |
|---|---|
| Calories | 388.5 |
| Fat | 20.4g |
| Cholesterol | 294.9mg |
| Sodium | 639.6mg |
| Carbohydrates | 32.4g |
| Protein | 18.2g |

## Ingredients

3 tbsps. frozen spinach, thawed
3 tbsps. artichoke hearts, minced
2 tsps. onions, minced
1 tsp. red bell pepper, minced
5 eggs
2 tbsps. milk
2 tbsps. heavy cream
1/4 cup shredded cheddar cheese

1/4 cup Monterey jack cheese, shredded
1 tbsp. parmesan cheese, shredded
1/4 tsp. salt
1 (8 ounce) packages Pillsbury Refrigerated Crescent Dinner Rolls
1 tbsp. butter, melted
1/4 cup asiago cheese, shredded

## Directions

1. First set the oven to 375F.

2. Add the spinach, onion, artichoke hearts and bell pepper in a bowl and combine well. Stir in 2 tbsp of water, use a plastic wrap to cover and pierce a few punctures in the wrap. Leave in the Microwave for 4 minutes on high.

3. Whisk 4 eggs in a second bowl. Stir in milk, cheddar cheese, cream, Parmesan, Jack Cheese and salt. Add the artichoke hearts, spinach, bell pepper and onion.

4. Cook the egg mixture in the Microwave for 35 seconds on high and combine well. Repeat this about 5 times until the eggs are scrambled.

5. Unravel and separate the dough into quarters.

6. Grease a few ramekins with melted butter. Place the dough in the bottom of each ramekin, then place a layer of egg mixture. Top up with 1 tbsp of shredded asiago cheese.

7. Whisk the balance egg in a 3rd bowl, brush the dough on each ramekin with the whisked egg mixture.

8. Cook in the oven for 30 minutes until the dough turns a slight brown. Transfer from oven and allow to cool for 10 minutes, then gently ease out the soufflé from each dish.

9. Serve warm.

# MENNONITE
# Pickled Eggs

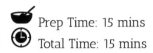
Prep Time: 15 mins
Total Time: 15 mins

Servings per Recipe: 6
Calories            186.9
Fat                 5.4g
Cholesterol         186.5mg
Sodium              511.7mg
Carbohydrates       26.0g
Protein             7.5g

## Ingredients

1 cup cider vinegar
1 cup beet juice
1/2 cup brown sugar
1 tsp. salt

6 hard-boiled eggs, shelled
1 (15 ounce) cans small round beets

## Directions

1. Add cider vinegar, beet juice, brown sugar and salt into a saucepan and boil for 6 minutes.
2. Allow the mixture to cool and fold over the hard-boiled eggs and round beets. Cover with plastic wrap and leave overnight in the refrigerator.
3. Slice the eggs into halves or into four and serve.
4. Enjoy.

# Ivy League
# Fried Eggs

🥣 Prep Time: 10 mins

🕐 Total Time: 17 mins

Servings per Recipe: 4

| | |
|---|---|
| Calories | 127.1 |
| Fat | 8.3g |
| Cholesterol | 186.0mg |
| Sodium | 75.1mg |
| Carbohydrates | 5.4g |
| Protein | 8.3g |

## Ingredients

1 tbsp. olive oil
1 tbsp. lemon juice
3 cups mushrooms, sliced
1 onion, chopped
2 - 4 garlic cloves, chopped
4 - 6 eggs

salt,
 ground black pepper,
1 tbsp. basil, chopped

## Directions

1. Add oil and lemon juice into a skillet and gently fry the onion, mushrooms and garlic until soft.

2. Stir in the eggs, adjust seasonings and allow to fry for a few minutes. At the time of setting gently flip over.

3. Fold the egg mixture into individual dishes and sprinkle chopped basil on top.

4. Enjoy.

# VENICE BEACH
# Brunch (Vidalia Scramble)

 Prep Time: 15 mins

Total Time: 30 mins

Servings per Recipe: 4

| | |
|---|---|
| Calories | 122.6 |
| Fat | 8.8g |
| Cholesterol | 212.9mg |
| Sodium | 114.6mg |
| Carbohydrates | 2.1g |
| Protein | 8.2g |

## Ingredients

4 large eggs
1 tbsp. olive oil
1/4 cup chopped sweet onion
1 medium plum tomato, diced
2 - 4 tbsps. chopped cilantro
kosher salt

black pepper, ground
1/4 cup shredded low-fat cheddar cheese

## Directions

1. Beat the eggs with 2 tbsps. of water if using eggs. This step is not required if you are using the egg substitute.
2. Heat olive oil in a frying pan.
3. Place the chopped sweet onion in the frying pan and sauté for 6 minutes.
4. Stir in cilantro, tomato, 1/2 tsp. of salt and pepper and increase the heat to high.
5. Cook for 2 minutes until the mixture is dry.
6. Combine the eggs gently with a non-stick spoon and cook for 4 minutes.
7. Allow to cook for 2 minutes more and sprinkle cheese on top.
8. Serve warm.
9. Enjoy.

# Scotch Eggs 101 (Breaded Hardboiled Eggs)

🍳 Prep Time: 15 mins
🕐 Total Time: 25 mins

Servings per Recipe: 4

| | |
|---|---|
| Calories | 314.6 |
| Fat | 20.8g |
| Cholesterol | 245.1mg |
| Sodium | 532.1mg |
| Carbohydrates | 12.9g |
| Protein | 17.2g |

## Ingredients

5 medium free-range eggs
225 g good quality sausage meat
2 tbsps. chopped herbs
1 tbsp. chopped spring onion, green onion
1/2 tsp. mace
1/4 tsp. mixed spice

2 tbsps. plain flour
75 g white breadcrumbs
salt and pepper
oil

## Directions

1. Place 4 eggs in cold water and allow to boil for 6 minutes. Rinse with cold water.

2. Whisk the remaining egg in a bowl. Place the plain four in another bowl and add seasonings. Place the white breadcrumbs in a 3rd bowl.

3. Place the sausage meat in a fourth bowl and stir in herbs, spring onions and mace. Using your hands combine the mixture well and separate into 4 parts. Peel the shells off the eggs and roll in the flour with seasonings. Flatten and wrap the sausage meat around each egg and dust with breadcrumbs.

4. Pour about 5cm oil into a skillet and heat well.

5. Add the eggs and leave until well browned for 12 minutes. Drain the excess fat and allow to cool.

6. The eggs can be kept refrigerated until ready to use.

7. Enjoy.

# WINNEBAGO
# Morning Wraps

Prep Time: 10 mins
Total Time: 25 mins

Servings per Recipe: 4
| | |
|---|---|
| Calories | 320.2 |
| Fat | 25.0g |
| Cholesterol | 158.2mg |
| Sodium | 562.8mg |
| Carbohydrates | 5.3g |
| Protein | 18.2g |

## Ingredients

1/4 cup A.1. Original Sauce, divided
1 tbsp. extra-virgin olive oil
1/2 tsp. granulated garlic
1/2 tsp. thyme leaves
8 ounces sirloin steaks
2 eggs, cracked and whisked
2 pinches sea salt
1/2 tsp. red pepper flakes

1 tbsp. butter
4 low-carb garden veggie wraps
1/4 cup mayonnaise
1/2 cup spinach leaves
4 cherry tomatoes, sliced
2 ounces goat cheese

## Directions

1. Place half of the sauce, garlic, olive oil and thyme leaves in a bowl and combine well. Coat the steak on all sides with sauce.

2. Place the steak on a heated frying pan and cook for 5 minutes per side until done. Take out from the heat and allow to cool for 6 minutes. Cut the steak into lean slices

3. Beat the eggs in a second bowl. Stir in pepper flakes and salt and combine well. Add butter to the frying pan and allow to heat. Allow the eggs to scramble for about 2 minutes.

4. Place the mayonnaise and balance sauce in a bowl.

5. Lay the wraps on a wooden chopping board. Drizzle the sauce mixture on the bottom of 1/3 of wraps. Follow with scrambled eggs, spinach leaves, goat cheese, tomatoes and steak slices. Fold the sides of the wrap and form a burrito.

6. Cover with a plastic wrap and leave until ready to serve.

7. Enjoy.

# *London*
# Tart Pie Shell

Prep Time: 15 mins
Total Time: 15 mins

Servings per Recipe: 1

| | |
|---|---|
| Calories | 4157.4 |
| Fat | 315.9g |
| Cholesterol | 186.0mg |
| Sodium | 1825.0mg |
| Carbohydrates | 286.5g |
| Protein | 45.0g |

## Ingredients

1 egg
3 cups flour
3/4 tsp. salt
1 1/2 cups cold vegetable shortening

1 tbsp. vinegar
5 tbsps. very cold water

## Directions

1. Add the flour and salt into a bowl and combine well.
2. Cut the cold vegetable shortening or lard with the use of a sharp knife to a similar size of peas.
3. Whisk the egg with vinegar and water in a bowl.
4. Stir in the egg mixture with the flour mix.
5. Form a ball.
6. Leave in the refrigerator for 2 hours.
7. Roll out the ball and use for a pie crust.
8. Enjoy.

# COMPLEX
# Toast

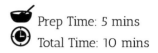 Prep Time: 5 mins

Total Time: 10 mins

Servings per Recipe: 2
| | |
|---|---|
| Calories | 1071.7 |
| Fat | 90.8g |
| Cholesterol | 632.9mg |
| Sodium | 861.3mg |
| Carbohydrates | 43.6g |
| Protein | 22.1g |

## Ingredients

4 hard-boiled eggs, chopped
1/4 cup butter
1/4 cup flour
1 1/2 cups cream

1/4 tsp. kosher salt
ground pepper,
4 slices bread, toasted

## Directions

1. Remove the shells from the eggs, cut into pieces and leave aside.
2. Place butter in a skillet and heat well.
3. Add the 1/4 cup of flour and allow to brown.
4. Gradually stir in the cream and combine well.
5. Remove from heat and stir in seasonings as desired.
6. Add the kept aside eggs.
7. Spread over the toasted slices of bread.
8. Enjoy.

# Dante's
# Tomato and Garlic Eggs

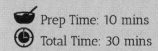 Prep Time: 10 mins

Total Time: 30 mins

Servings per Recipe: 4
| | |
|---|---|
| Calories | 256.8 |
| Fat | 16.8g |
| Cholesterol | 373.1mg |
| Sodium | 196.4mg |
| Carbohydrates | 12.2g |
| Protein | 15.1g |

## Ingredients

1 clove crushed garlic
2 tbsps. olive oil
2 cups canned tomato puree
4 basil leaves, torn into pieces
1 pinch dried oregano
salt and pepper

8 large eggs
1 tbsp. parmesan cheese

## Directions

1. Pour the oil into a frying pan and sauté the garlic for about 3 minutes.
2. Stir in the tomato, basil and seasonings.
3. Allow the mixture to simmer for about 16 minutes until the sauce becomes thick in consistency.
4. Crack the egg and place in a bowl.
5. Form a small well in the sauce with a wooden spatula.
6. Add the egg into the tomato sauce.
7. Follow with the rest of the eggs.
8. Sprinkle cheese on top.
9. Cover with lid and cook for 4 minutes until the eggs are cooked.
10. Serve warm.
11. Enjoy.

# VERNA'S
# Spud Cakes

Prep Time: 15 mins
Total Time: 35 mins

Servings per Recipe: 6
Calories            430.8
Fat                 38.4g
Cholesterol         349.7mg
Sodium              353.8mg
Carbohydrates       1.0g
Protein             19.9g

## Ingredients

1/2 cup olive oil
24 ounces Simply Potatoes Traditional
Mashed Potatoes
20 ounces simply potatoes southwest-

style hash browns
8 ounces sharp cheddar cheese
10 eggs, poached

## Directions

1. Pour the oil into a frying pan and allow to heat well.
2. Divide the mashed potatoes into ten portions.
3. Insert the hash browns into a small bowl.
4. Stir in a piece of mashed potatoes into the hash browns and press slightly. Place the block of cheese in the middle. Fold over the potatoes and seal. Turn to the other side and cover with hash browns.
5. Place the cakes in warm oil and allow to brown on both side.
6. Cook the eggs and place on the potato cakes.
7. Enjoy.

# Country
# Egg Sandwiches

🍳 Prep Time: 10 mins
🕐 Total Time: 20 mins

Servings per Recipe: 2
| | |
|---|---|
| Calories | 529.7 |
| Fat | 16.0g |
| Cholesterol | 0.0mg |
| Sodium | 661.4mg |
| Carbohydrates | 80.9g |
| Protein | 16.2g |

## Ingredients

2 tbsps. olive oil
1 red bell pepper, strips
1 onion, chopped
1 cup Egg Beaters egg substitute
4 -6 slices edam cheese, sliced

4 slices country bread, toasted
salt and pepper

## Directions

1. Pour the oil into a frying pan and allow to heat. Sauté the onion for 3 minutes until tender.
2. Toss in the red bell pepper strips and leave to cook for 12 minutes.
3. Adjust seasonings by adding salt and pepper.
4. Stir in the eggs to the frying pan; stir continuously and leave for 3 minutes.
5. Spread the egg mix on 2 slices of toasted country bread. Place the cheese on top and sandwich with the balance toast.
6. Slice each sandwich into two and serve.
7. Enjoy.

# LIVERPOOL
# Eggs

Prep Time: 10 mins
Total Time: 30 mins

Servings per Recipe: 6
| | |
|---|---|
| Calories | 294.8 |
| Fat | 21.9g |
| Cholesterol | 411.5mg |
| Sodium | 375.9mg |
| Carbohydrates | 1.2g |
| Protein | 21.9g |

## Ingredients

2 cups mild cheddar cheese, grated
12 eggs
salt

seasoned pepper

## Directions

1. Grease six ramekins with butter and place about 1/4 cup of cheese on each ramekin.
2. Crack the eggs and gently place on the cheese ensuring not to damage the yolk. Place 2 eggs on each ramekin.
3. Sprinkle the balance grated cheese on top and adjust seasonings.
4. Cook in an oven for 25 minutes at a temperature of 325F until the eggs are done.
5. Can be served with buttered toast.
6. Enjoy.

# *Protein*
# Bread Machine

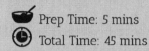 Prep Time: 5 mins

Total Time: 45 mins

Servings per Recipe: 1

| | |
|---|---|
| Calories | 2150.0 |
| Fat | 52.6g |
| Cholesterol | 311.7mg |
| Sodium | 3996.1mg |
| Carbohydrates | 358.7g |
| Protein | 57.4g |

## Ingredients

1 egg
1 cup milk
3 cups flour
1 1/2 tsps. salt
4 1/2 tbsps. sugar

3 tbsps. butter
2 1/2 tsps. yeast

## Directions

1. Place all the ingredients in a bread pan and combine well.

2. Switch to white bread mode, but leave a bit more time for rising.

3. Enjoy.

# ONTARIO
# Egg Bake

Prep Time: 4 mins
Total Time: 23 mins

Servings per Recipe: 1
Calories              268.1
Fat                   24.6g
Cholesterol           245.8mg
Sodium                330.9mg
Carbohydrates         1.1g
Protein               10.5g

## Ingredients

1 tbsp. butter, melted
2 tbsps. parmesan cheese, grated
1 large egg

1 tbsp. whipping cream

## Directions

1. Before you do anything set the oven to 350F.
2. Grease a ramekin with butter and sprinkle 1 tbsp of grated cheese on top.
3. Crack an egg to the ramekin and top up with the whipping cream.
4. Cover with the balance grated cheese on top.
5. Cook in the oven for 12 minutes until the whites are hardened.
6. Serve warm.
7. Enjoy.

# Athenian City
# Bread Machine

Prep Time: 5 mins
Total Time: 10 mins

Servings per Recipe: 2
| | |
|---|---|
| Calories | 148.4 |
| Fat | 11.8g |
| Cholesterol | 235.8mg |
| Sodium | 299.7mg |
| Carbohydrates | 1.1g |
| Protein | 8.9g |

## Ingredients

1 egg
1 cup milk
3 cups flour
1 1/2 tsps. salt
4 1/2 tbsps. sugar

3 tbsps. butter
2 1/2 tsps. yeast

## Directions

1. Place margarine or butter in a frying pan and heat well.
2. Whisk the eggs and stir into the frying pan.
3. Stir in the cheese and allow the eggs to scramble for a few minutes.
4. Adjust seasonings.
5. Enjoy.

# TORTILLA
# Brunch Skillet

Prep Time: 3 mins
Total Time: 8 mins

Servings per Recipe: 2

| | |
|---|---|
| Calories | 460.0 |
| Fat | 30.7g |
| Cholesterol | 637.7mg |
| Sodium | 242.8mg |
| Carbohydrates | 23.6g |
| Protein | 22.3g |

## Ingredients

6 eggs
3 tbsps. milk
4 corn tortillas, cut into triangles
2 tbsps. oil
salt

shredded cheddar cheese
salsa

## Directions

1. Break the 6 eggs into a large bowl and combine with milk.
2. Whisk the mixture using a fork.
3. Place 2 tbsp of oil in a frying pan and allow to heat.
4. Fold in the tortillas and add a dash of salt.
5. Allow the tortillas to fry for about 3 minutes.
6. Stir in the egg mix over the tortillas. Add more salt if required.
7. Fold the mixture with a wooden spoon until the mixture is cooked ensuring not to overcook.
8. Remove from heat and sprinkle cheese on top.
9. Cover the frying pan with a cover and allow the cheese to melt for about 3 minutes.
10. Serve with salsa.
11. Enjoy.

# *Eggs* Calabasas

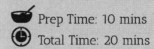 Prep Time: 10 mins

Total Time: 20 mins

Servings per Recipe: 3
| | |
|---|---|
| Calories | 263.4 |
| Fat | 18.8g |
| Cholesterol | 372.0mg |
| Sodium | 149.1mg |
| Carbohydrates | 9.8g |
| Protein | 14.1g |

## Ingredients

2 tbsps. oil
1 onion, chopped
1 bell pepper, chopped
2 garlic cloves, minced
2 tomatoes, seeded and chopped

6 eggs, lightly beaten
salt and pepper

## Directions

1. Pour the oil into a frying pan and heat well. Sauté the onion, garlic and bell pepper for 5 minutes until the onion becomes soft.

2. Stir in the chopped tomatoes and allow to cook for 5 minutes.

3. Lower the heat, toss in the eggs and seasonings. Stir the eggs and allow to scramble until cooked through.

4. Can be served with fresh cheese, arepas or slices of bread.

5. Enjoy.

# FLAMINGO
# Wraps

Prep Time: 10 mins
Total Time: 25 mins

Servings per Recipe: 6
Calories          456.0
Fat               23.5g
Cholesterol       277.9mg
Sodium            815.1mg
Carbohydrates     38.2g
Protein           21.5g

## Ingredients

1 tbsp. vegetable oil
1 sweet red pepper, chopped
8 eggs
2 tbsps. low-fat milk
1/4 tsp. salt

1/4 tsp. pepper
1 1/2 cups cheddar cheese, shredded
6 tortillas, whole wheat, flax

## Directions

1. Pour oil into a frying pan and heat well; sauté the chopped red pepper for 4 minutes.

2. Place the milk, eggs, salt and pepper in a bowl and beat together; fold in the mixture to the frying pan and leave until cooked and the mixture becomes dry.

3. Top up each tortilla center with shredded cheese; spread about 1/3 cup of the egg mixture on top. Fold the tortilla over the mixture in the shape of a square. Place the square with seam facing downwards in the frying pan and cook for about 5 minutes.

4. Enjoy.

# *Jade*
# Garden Egg Foo Yung

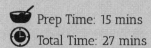 Prep Time: 15 mins

Total Time: 27 mins

Servings per Recipe: 2
| | |
|---|---|
| Calories | 384.1 |
| Fat | 28.0g |
| Cholesterol | 558.0mg |
| Sodium | 1023.4mg |
| Carbohydrates | 11.2g |
| Protein | 22.6g |

## Ingredients

4 tbsps. canola oil
1/4 cup onion, chopped
2 cups cabbage, shredded
6 eggs
1 tbsp. soy sauce
2 tbsps. sesame oil
1/2 tsp. garlic powder

1/4 tsp. salt
1/8 tsp. ground black pepper
1 cup bean sprouts
1 cup cooked small shrimp

## Directions

1. Pour 2 tbsps. of canola oil into a frying pan, and sauté the 1/4 cup chopped onion and shredded cabbage until soft.

2. Take out from the heat and drain off the fat. Keep the tempered cabbage and onion aside.

3. Place eggs, sesame oil, soy sauce, onion mixture, sprouts and spices in a bowl and beat well.

4. Pour the balance oil into a skillet and heat well.

5. Fold in 4 oz. of the mixture into the hot skillet. Place the small shrimp on top.

6. Keep in the heat for 4 minutes until the corners brown slightly.

7. Enjoy.

# TATOR TOT
# Lunch Box

Prep Time: 10 mins
Total Time: 30 mins

Servings per Recipe: 6
| | |
|---|---|
| Calories | 240.0 |
| Fat | 18.7g |
| Cholesterol | 386.8mg |
| Sodium | 229.7mg |
| Carbohydrates | 0.9g |
| Protein | 16.0g |

## Ingredients

50 - 60 tater tots
12 eggs
2 tbsps. vegetable oil

12 tbsps. shredded cheddar cheese

## Directions

1. Before you do anything set the oven to 375F.
2. Keep the 1 pack of tater tots in the room temperature for 1 to 2 minutes.
3. Brush a muffin tray with 12 cups with 2 tbsps. of vegetable oil.
4. Place 5 tots in each muffin cup.
5. Botch the tots with the use of a spoon so it will be at the bottom of each muffin cup.
6. Sprinkle 1 tbsp of cheese on top.
7. Insert the muffin tray into the oven and let it cook for 6 minutes.
8. Remove from the oven; crack one egg into each muffin cup.
9. Leave in the oven for 16 - 22 minutes until the eggs are firm.
10. Take out from the oven.
11. Loosen the sides and bottom of each cup using a non-stick spoon.
12. Serve warm.
13. Enjoy.

# Moscow
# Egg Boats

Prep Time: 10 mins
Total Time: 10 mins

Servings per Recipe: 8

| | |
|---|---|
| Calories | 60.0 |
| Fat | 3.9g |
| Cholesterol | 106.9mg |
| Sodium | 57.6mg |
| Carbohydrates | 2.8g |
| Protein | 3.3g |

## Ingredients

4 hard-boiled eggs, sliced in half
1 very small onion, chopped
1 tsp. olive oil
1 tsp. paprika

2 tbsps. mayonnaise
1 -1 1/2 tbsp. lemon juice
salt and pepper,

## Directions

1. Pour the olive oil into a skillet and temper the small onion. You could skip this step if you wish.
2. Separate the egg yolks and insert them into a bowl.
3. Botch the yolks and mix with the rest of the ingredients.
4. Fold in the mixture into the egg whites and leave in the refrigerator.
5. Enjoy.

# EGGS
# Sacramento

Prep Time: 15 mins
Total Time: 18 mins

Servings per Recipe: 24
| | |
|---|---|
| Calories | 60.1 |
| Fat | 4.6g |
| Cholesterol | 81.8mg |
| Sodium | 64.7mg |
| Carbohydrates | 1.8g |
| Protein | 3.1g |

## Ingredients

1 dozen egg
2 medium ripe California avocados
2 tbsps. onions, minced
1 tbsp. lemon juice
1/4 tsp. salt

1/2 tsp. paprika
6 black olives, diced

## Directions

1. Place the dozen eggs in boiling water and heat for 4 minutes.
2. Remove the shells and cut the eggs into two along the length.
3. Extract the egg yolks from the whites and lay the whites on a serving dish.
4. Botch the egg yolks and avocados together.
5. Stir in the onions, salt and lemon juice.
6. Stuff the egg yolk mixture into the whites.
7. Serve sprinkled with olives and paprika.
8. Enjoy.

# New England
# Egg Salad

🍲 Prep Time: 10 mins
🕐 Total Time: 10 mins

Servings per Recipe: 6
| | |
|---|---|
| Calories | 178.2 |
| Fat | 8.6g |
| Cholesterol | 240.7mg |
| Sodium | 341.3mg |
| Carbohydrates | 2.9g |
| Protein | 21.9g |

## Ingredients

14 -15 ounces canned salmon, flaked
6 hard-boiled eggs, peeled and chopped
1/2 cup chopped onion
1/2 cucumber, peeled, seeded and chopped
1 1/2 tsps. Dijon mustard

1/2-3/4 cup mayonnaise
1/8 tsp. black pepper
1/2-3/4 tsp. dried tarragon
1/4 tsp. paprika
salt

## Directions

1. Place salmon, eggs, onion, cucumber, mustard, mayonnaise, pepper, tarragon and paprika in a bowl and combine well.

2. Add salt .

3. Leave in the refrigerator to chill prior to serving.

4. Enjoy.

# CINNAMON
# Pinwheel Bread

Prep Time: 3 hrs
Total Time: 3 hrs 25 mins

Servings per Recipe: 10
Calories          338.6
Fat               6.2g
Cholesterol       46.8mg
Sodium            187.7mg
Carbohydrates     61.3g
Protein           8.7g

## Ingredients

4 3/4-5 1/4 cups all-purpose flour
1 package yeast
1 1/3 cups milk
3 tbsps. sugar
3 tbsps. margarine

1/2 tsp. salt
2 eggs
1/2 cup sugar
2 tsps. cinnamon

## Directions

1. Place 2 cups of the all-purpose flour and yeast in a bowl and mix well.
2. Pour 3 tbsps. of milk into a pot and heat well.
3. Stir in the margarine, sugar and salt and leave until the margarine becomes soft and melted.
4. Fold the mixture into the 1st bowl; add eggs.
5. Whisk for 32 seconds using a mixer on low speed.
6. Whisk for 4 minutes on high speed.
7. Fold in the balance flour to the mixture.
8. Dust a wooden board with flour and place the dough on it
9. Knead well for about 10 minutes.
10. Grease a bowl with butter and place the dough in it.
11. Cover with a wet cloth and leave at room temperature.
12. Knead the dough and once again and place on the floured board.
13. Make two portions out of the dough.
14. Cover and allow to rise for 12 minutes.
15. Spread out the dough with a rolling pin to 12x7" rectangles.
16. Brush a sprinkling of water on top.
17. Roll up and secure the ends and the corners.

18. Grease bread pans and place the dough seam side facing downwards.
19. Cover with a damp cloth and allow to rise.
20. Leave in the oven for 35 minutes at a temperature of 375F.
21. During the last 12 minutes of cooking, ensure to cover loosely.
22. Gently take out from the pans and allow to cool.
23. Enjoy.

# IRONBOUND
# Tortillas

Prep Time: 5 mins
Total Time: 25 mins

Servings per Recipe: 6
| | |
|---|---|
| Calories | 816.8 |
| Fat | 45.4g |
| Cholesterol | 261.0mg |
| Sodium | 1782.8mg |
| Carbohydrates | 62.7g |
| Protein | 36.5g |

## Ingredients

1 lb. chorizo sausage, broken up
6 -8 large eggs, lightly beaten
1 large onion, chopped
6 large flour tortillas, browned in a pan
1/2 cup grated Monterey jack cheese

sour cream
hot sauce
chopped avocado

## Directions

1. Place the onion and broken up sausage in a skillet and sauté until the onion becomes soft.
2. Whisk the eggs and stir into the sausage mixture.
3. Brush sour cream on the pan-fried tortilla and serve with tortillas; sprinkle cheese and chopped avocado on top.
4. If required add more hot sauce and sour cream.
5. Enjoy.

# *Sonoma*
# Sandwich

🥣 Prep Time: 15 mins

🕐 Total Time: 20 mins

Servings per Recipe: 3
| | |
|---|---|
| Calories | 541.4 |
| Fat | 15.7g |
| Cholesterol | 187.3mg |
| Sodium | 950.6mg |
| Carbohydrates | 78.6g |
| Protein | 22.4g |

## Ingredients

3 large hard-boiled eggs, peeled and chopped

3 tbsps. white onions, chopped

2 tbsps. parsley leaves, chopped

1 tsp. dill, chopped

1/2 tsp. Dijon mustard

2 tsps. mayonnaise

1 large Hass avocado, diced

1/4 tsp. sea salt

1/16 tsp. black pepper

6 - 8 slices brioche bread, lightly toasted

4 slices Monterey Jack cheese

## Directions

1. Place the eggs, parsley, onion, Dijon, dill and mayonnaise in a bowl and combine well.

2. Fold in the Hass avocado, adjust seasonings and combine well.

3. Take the slices of bread and slightly fry them in a pan until lightly toasted.

4. Place the avocado and egg mixture on the bread, place a cheese slice and sandwich with another bread slice.

5. Enjoy.

# CHINESE
# Scrambled Eggs

Prep Time: 3 mins
Total Time: 18 mins

Servings per Recipe: 4
Calories             95.0
Fat                  6.0g
Cholesterol          186.0mg
Sodium               74.1mg
Carbohydrates        3.3g
Protein              6.8g

## Ingredients

2 tomatoes, diced
4 free range eggs
olive oil
1 tsp. sesame oil
2 tsps. rice vinegar

1 tsp. cornstarch
green onion, chopped,
salt and pepper

## Directions

1. Whisk the eggs; adjust seasonings and stir in the green onion white part.
2. Combine well.
3. Pour sesame oil into a skillet and heat well.
4. Fold in the egg mix.
5. Scramble the egg mixture and leave until the eggs are cooked for about 1 minute.
6. Remove the eggs from the skillet.
7. Pour olive oil into the skillet and add the tomatoes.
8. Add salt, pepper, sugar and rice vinegar and cook the tomatoes.
9. Stir in the green onion green part.
10. Add the cornstarch with 1 tsp of water in a bowl and combine well.
11. Pour the mixture over the tomatoes and combine well.
12. Serve warm.
13. Enjoy.

# Westminster
# Sandwich

Prep Time: 10 mins
Total Time: 10 mins

Servings per Recipe: 1
Calories          155.3
Fat               8.2g
Cholesterol       194.6mg
Sodium            201.6mg
Carbohydrates     11.6g
Protein           9.8g

## Ingredients

1 tbsp. reduced-fat cream cheese
1 tsp. whole grain mustard
1/2 tsp. chopped dill
2 slices whole-grain rye bread, toasted
1 large hard-boiled egg, sliced

2 tomatoes, slices
1 pinch salt and pepper

## Directions

1. Combine the mustard, cream cheese and dill in a bowl. Slightly toast the bread and coat the bread with the cream cheese mixture.

2. Place tomato, egg, salt and pepper on one slice. Top up with the other bread slice.

3. Enjoy.

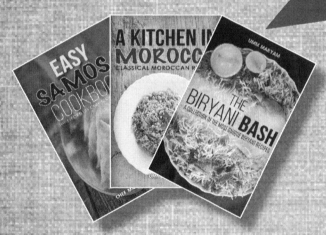

Printed in Great Britain
by Amazon